A User's Guide to PARENTHOOD

Wisdom for Facing the Trials of Raising Kids

Jo Elder and M.I. Wiser

Ilustrations by Janora Bayot

One More Press
Lake Oswego, Oregon

Printed in the United States of America

Copyright © 1992 by Jo Elder & M.I. Wiser
Revised edition © 1993 by Jo Elder & M.I. Wiser

Library of Congress Cataloging-in-Publication Data
Elder, Jo -
    A user's guide to parenthood:"wisdom for facing the trials of
raising kids" / by Jo Elder and M.I. Wiser; illustrations by Janora Bayot
        p. cm.
    Includes index.
    ISBN 0-941361-99-3 : $6.50
        1. Parenting — United States.   2. Child rearing — United States.
I. Wiser, M.I.,-   II. Title.
HQ769.E54   1992
649'.1—dc20

                                                                    92-27868
                                                                          CIP

One More Press
P.O. Box 1885
Lake Oswego, OR 97035
(503) 697-7964

A User's Guide to Parenthood

Introduction

 oasters come with instructions. So do cameras, can openers and computers. Even with an electric toothbrush, you're not entirely on your own— there's a nifty little booklet that tells you how to operate the thing. (And we won't even mention the encyclopedia of directions that came with your VCR!)

But what about children? That's an entirely different story. They come to you with no guarantees or instructions. The stork delivers them to your doorstep with not one word of advice pinned to their diapers. Your mother, of course, will try to make up for the deficit. ("Now you know what I had to put up with all those years!") But even so, as a parent, you sail into the vast, uncharted waters of parenthood all on your own.

"If only kids came with a set of instructions," you say. Well, now they do! Here's the help and encouragement all parents need, whether they're new to the job as first-time parents or dealing with the special needs of older children and teens. In this small but effective **User's Guide to Parenthood**, you'll find words of wisdom and encouragement from two parents who have raised (and are still raising) an assortment of offspring. Along the way, we veteran parents have earned the appropriate medals and stripes, while surviving the whole experience with surprisingly few scars.

It hasn't always been easy. There have been plenty of times when we've wished for a set of instructions to guide us through a particularly trying experience. There have been times when what we've really needed was a pat on the back and confirmation that we were headed in the right direction. So in writing this book, we've shared with you our thoughts, suggestions and observations, laced with the lighthearted humor you'll need to encourage and reassure you as you work your way through parenthood.

Jo Elder
M.I. Wiser

To our children,
who've given us happiness, love,
and plenty of reasons to write this book.

1 ❤ Accept your children as they are, not as you wish them to be, and you will help them to become their best.

2 ❤ There's nothing quite so challenging as raising children. Just as soon as you teach them to talk you have to begin instructing them in the art of being quiet.

3 ❤ All children need love, but none so much as those who don't seem to deserve it.

4 ❤ *"Nevertheless"* is a handy phrase that keeps a conversation on track when teenagers try to sidetrack you with remarks, looks, stances and other irritating behaviors.

5 ❤ *"Parents who are afraid to put their foot down usually have children who step on their toes."*

Oriental saying

6 ❤ You'll make reading important to your children if you begin reading to them when they are infants and never stop.

7 ❤ Allow your children to tell white lies and they will most likely grow up color-blind.

8 ❤ Make sure staying home sick from school isn't fun. If you don't allow TV or out-of-bed activities, children will find staying home boring and be less eager to miss school.

9 ❤ To a small child, all problems are big problems.

10 ❤ Before your children start a new school, take them to visit the school. Explore the building, have a picnic in the school yard and meet the staff. This will make the first day more comfortable.

11 ❤ Adolescents soon believe they know everything; it's not until they are raising their own children that they realize just how little they know.

12 ❤ Encourage your children to set safe challenges for themselves. Example: to read all the books written by their favorite author.

13 ❤ Set limits on the kind of cooking your children are allowed to do when you are not present.

14 ❤ Plant a tree for each child and care for it together.

15 ❤ Take your children with you when you vote.

16 ❤ Teach your children how to administer simple first aid.

17 ❤ There's a definite connection between how your children are dressed and how they act. Don't send your children to school dressed for play; send them in an attire that promotes the business of learning.

18 ♥ Go to a parade.

19 ♥ Write your teenager a note about his or her virtues and strengths.

20 ♥ Let each family member name a favorite food. One night have a "Crazy Quilt" meal serving everyone's favorite dish.

21 ❤ Plant flowers together.

22 ❤ Share a sunrise with your child.

23 ❤ Start family traditions.

24 ❤ Never leave young children unattended in a pool area, even if they are not in the water.

25 ❤ Make it a daily habit to ask your children what they enjoyed most about each day.

26 ❤ Have the courage to set limits for your children. Let them know what you will not allow and you will give them the courage to say no to choices that can bring them harm.

27 ❤ Always know what your child is wearing. If, for some reason, your child is late or missing, you won't waste any time coming up with a detailed description.

28 ❤ Never call your mother to complain
about what the kids have done.
She'll only point out that you did the
same, or worse.

29 ❤ Forgive.

30 ❤ Always kiss your kids goodnight
and good morning.

31 ❤ By the time our children finally learn to pick up after themselves, most of us are picking up after our grandchildren.

32 ❤ Put family photos near your children's beds so that they have a sense of belonging. Let them pick out the photos.

33 ❤ If you show appreciation to your children when they do something special for you, they will learn to show appreciation to others. As parents however, you will most likely have to wait until your children have families of their own before they will show you much appreciation.

34 ❤ Teach your kids to respect all living creatures.

35 ❤ Exposure to TV violence increases a child's tolerance for aggressive and antisocial acts.

36 ❤ Ask your doctor to teach you the Heimlich Maneuver.

37 ❤ Make your children carry identification whenever they leave home. It should include their name, address and emergency phone numbers.

38 ❤ A lot of parents expect their kids to have things they never had, like straight A's and perfect manners.

39 ❤ No matter how many children you have, once you start asking who's responsible for misdeeds, you'll find you have one more named *Nobody* who did all the mischief.

40 ❤ Sometimes it is better to overlook the small problems and save your energy for the big problems.

41 ❤ Shy and only children benefit from spending time with other children their age. If you create opportunities for them to make friends you will be teaching them how to get along with others.

42 ❤ Parental intuition is not always infallible.

43 ❤ *"To bring up a child in the way he should go, travel that way yourself once in a while."*

Josh Billings

44 ❤ Many of your child's behavior problems are learned – either from seeing someone else do it or because of the response it gets.

45 ❤ By the time children enter elementary school they will often have embarrassed their parents; by the time they leave high school they will often be embarrassed by their parents.

46 ❤ Heredity is something parents with very bright children believe in.

47 ❤ "Time-out" works well for fighting, tantrums and destructive acts.

48 ❤ Select a time-out location where you can send your children when they practice inappropriate behavior. Use a timer to keep track of the time; one minute for each year of age is an appropriate time-out.

49 ❤ Make sure time-out immediately follows the misbehavior.

50 ❤ If your children leave the time-out location before their time is up, teach them that you will then reset the time-out clock.

51 ❤ Don't stay angry.

52 ❤ *"When two elephants fight, it is the grass underneath that suffers"*
African proverb

53 ❤ If you have a fight with your child, make the first move to reconcile. Hug him or her and say I love you. Even if the child pushes you away, it will begin to heal the wounds.

54 ❤ If you think you're embarrassed when your children tell lies, wait until they begin sharing the family's intimate truths.

55 ❤ Nothing will put parents on the edge of their seat faster than having their child begin to relate a family incident to one of the neighbors.

56 ❤ Teach your children that you will always love them no matter how they look. Don't let them feel they are only as good as they perceive their body to be.

57 ❤ Never make fun of your kids.

58 ❤ Don't compare your children.

59 ❤ Encourage your children and they will grow up to become confident adults.

60 ❤ If children live with criticism they learn to condemn.

61 ❤ Help your children learn how to set attainable goals.

62 ❤ Always remember that you must not only educate a child in how to make a living but also teach him or her how to have a happy life.

63 ❤ A college education costs less than a lifetime of ignorance.

64 ❤ Teach your children to recycle.

65 ❤ *"You should not say it is not good. You should say you do not like it; and then, you know, you're perfectly safe."*

J.M. Whistler

66 ♥ Ask your children every day what they learned at school.

67 ♥ Acknowledge each new skill and success your child gains, no matter how small.

68 ♥ Every child should have a library card.

69 ❤ Don't just jump on your child about poor grades, take on the responsibility of teaching them how to study.

70 ❤ Encourage your children to develop their mechanical skills by letting them take apart junk appliances or clocks.

71 ❤ Guide your children in choosing a career, and respect the choice they make.

72 ❤ Keep telling your kids what is right and wrong. Even if they don't act like they're listening, your words will pop into their heads just when they need it.

73 ❤ Sometimes you have to pull a few wires to help your children get a better education: like unplugging the TV, radio or stereo.

74 ❤ Make firm telephone rules **before** your children become teenagers.

75 ❤ Enjoy each day.

76 ❤ Help your children design a family flag or crest.

77 ❤ Look for four-leaf clovers.

78 ❤ Trace your family tree.

79 ❤ Playing with your children will keep you young.

80 ❤ Make the creation of a family time capsule an annual event. In later years, looking back will create yet another family tradition, one you can share with your grandchildren.

81 ❤ It's the quality of the time you spend with your child, not the quantity that really counts.

82 ❤ Help your beginning readers to create a book about themselves. They can put in the photos and tell you what to print below each one. Make it a book they can read and reread.

83 ❤ Encourage older children to keep a journal.

84 ❤ Keep lots of reading material around. Books, magazines and newspapers that are easily accessible invite reading.

85 ❤ Children learn through observations. If they see abuse, deceit and belittlement of others they will develop those characteristics.

86 ❤ To help your teenagers understand thoughtful spending involve them in price and value comparisons at the grocery store.

87 ❤ Ask your teenagers their opinion whenever possible.

88 ❤ Children learn by example.

89 ❤ Allow your teenagers to dress as they please, within limits, when they're with their friends. Save the clothing battles for school and other important occasions.

90 ❤ Extra words just cause blank stares. Be short and to the point, especially when talking to teenagers.

91 ❤ Don't let your teenagers' protests stop you from taking them on a family outing. You will often find out later that this outing provided one of their lasting good time memories.

92 ❤ Time will alleviate most of your teenager's problems.

93 ❤ Adolescence is a time of rapid change. Between the ages of 13 and 18 a parent ages 20 years.

94 ❤ Teenagers like to hear about things their parents worried about as teens. It gives them the confidence that they too will make it through these trying times.

95 ❤ The best way to keep your teenager home is to make your home a pleasant place to hang out, and your car keys inaccessible.

96 ❤ Attend to the individuality and "differentness" of each child and you will develop each child's personality and potential to the fullest.

97 ❤ When your teenagers open up and tells you about something that has happened, resist the urge to reprimand or lecture. If you don't, you will lose their confidence. Save the sermon for another day.

98 ❤ If children live with shame they learn to feel guilty.

99 ❤ Kids are natural impersonators. They will act like their parents do, in spite of everything their parents say about good manners and behavior.

100 ❤ If parents smoke, chances are their children will smoke.

101 ❤ Take your kid's feelings seriously.

102 ❤ The best way a father can show his children how to be a thoughtful individual is to show them how much he cares about them and their mother by being an equal participant in their rearing.

103 ❤ Parents should always work as a team.

104 ❤ The use of natural and logical
consequences will help your children
become responsible for their own
behavior.

105 ❤ Punishment demands obedience; logical consequences permit choice.

106 ❤ Children learn to do things that lead to positive consequences. Reinforce or reward their good actions.

107 ❤ Logical consequences allow children to make responsible decisions.

108 ❤ A well-adjusted adult is one who as a child learned many ways to handle life's stresses, developed many skills and had numerous interests.

109 ❤ Correct children when they put themselves down. Use active listening, then respond with a positive statement.

110 ❤ Enforce mandatory rules, ones your children must obey, by clearly stating each rule and then consistently following up on those rules.

111 ❤ Be clear on what chores you expect your child to do, and make sure your child knows that doing these chores is mandatory.

112 ❤ If you do not follow up on rules, kids will make them optional.

113 ❤ Let your children make some rules for themselves.

114 ❤ Rules should always be rules, whether set by the parents or kids. Rules are never optional.

115 ❤ Stop worrying that your teenagers
will never grow up. Remember,
when they grow up they'll be gone.

116 ❤ Sometimes the most annoying thing
about children is that they're so
childish.

117 ❤ Never give up on a child.

118 ❤ Teenagers defy their parents for the purely selfish reason that they are caught up in the pleasure of the moment. This allows them to brush aside any thought of consequence.

119 ❤ No child is ever old enough to be convinced that he or she should have known better.

120 ❤ Negotiating with your children allows them to collaborate on their own destiny and feel as though they share control with their parents.

121 ❤ Treat your kids exactly as you'd like to be treated.

122 ❤ You don't have to win every battle.

123 ❤ Would the son or daughter you were be proud of the parent you are today?

124 ❤ Your child's strengths won't always be the same as yours. A parent's responsibility is to help his or her children develop their own interests and abilities, even when they differ.

125 ❤ The reason new babies are so adorable is to make sure the parents will tolerate their unexplained outbursts until they outgrow them.

126 ❤ Nearly half of all babies are fussy, or downright cranky, for the first few months of their lives.

127 ❤ Fussy babies are often sensitive to cold. Try turning up the heat in their room. You can also put them on their stomach to conserve body heat.

128 ❤ Being a baby is a time of frustration while mastering numerous skills. Fussy spells often mark your baby's reach for new skills.

129 ❤ Nursing mothers should not give their baby a pacifier until they are at least two months old. It tends to make them lazy nursers as it encourages the use of different muscles and leads to confusion.

130 ❤ A smile is one language even a baby understands.

131 ❤ Toddlers are often poisoned by eating common plants. Know what's in your house and yard, and supervise the area or remove any harmful plants.

132 ❤ You won't always be your kid's hero, make the most of those early years.

133 ❤ At age five children are eager to learn but their attention span is generally very short. This makes it important to teach the same lesson over and over, with patience.

134 ❤ Never interview a potential baby-sitter until after you have personally checked his or her references.

135 ❤ If you make it your job to help your children learn to read before they enter school, their teachers can concentrate on teaching them the art of reading to learn.

136 ❤ Children who see their parents reading will develop a love for reading.

137 ❤ If you're about to take a trip, get your children a book that will involve them in your destination.

138 ❤ Never pass a historical marker without stopping; each is an education in itself.

139 ❤ Spend time alone with each child.

140 ❤ Be a good loser; kids will learn from you.

141 ❤ Give your children, and yourself, an occasional day off from chores.

142 ❤ If your children like rollerblading (or another hot new sport) give it a try.

143 ❤ Get your kids a dog; it'll teach you a
new set of responsibilities.

144 ❤ Check out summer camps the year before you will be sending your children. Make a personal visit to the camp, and after camp is over, talk to parents whose children have attended the camp.

145 ❤ Give your kids the gift of music; most schools offer free programs.

146 ❤ Leave a love note in your children's lunch bag or on their mirror.

147 ❤ If you approve of your children they will like themselves.

148 ❤ Mark Twain once said *"I can live for two months on a good compliment."* So can your children.

149 ❤ Let your children know that you will love them no matter what happens.

150 ❤ Take joy in your child's choices, even if it's not what you wanted for their future.

151 ❤ Tell your child what you admire or appreciate about him or her.

152 ❤ Tell your kids how beautiful you think they are.

153 ❤ Learning about your children's interests will establish an intimacy that will last a lifetime. Take the time to ask them about their favorite recording artist, book, movie and activities.

154 ❤ If you want good manners in a restaurant, set a good table at home.

155 ❤ Limit your childrens' TV time to two hours a day or less.

156 ❤ Use TV as a way to encourage reading. Practice the "let's read more about it" approach to TV viewing.

157 ❤ Home is where children learn the most about financial attitudes. Make sure it's not just TV commercials that are doing the teaching.

158 ❤ Talk about commercials and the power of persuasion. Explain how the advertiser's job is to convince us we can't live without the product.

159 ♥ Teach your child the value of a dollar.

160 ♥ Start giving your children coins to spend at age three. This is a good way to start teaching them how money is traded for goods.

161 ♥ Teach your kids to save.

162 ❤ When your children are 4 or 5, allow them to handle coins and point out each coin's difference in both size and value.

163 ❤ Children should receive an unconditional allowance based on their age and your financial condition.

164 ❤ Try to let your children spend their allowance as they wish. You may not always approve of their choices but sometimes poorly spent money teaches a lesson all its own.

165 ❤ Teaching children that their allowance is their part of the family income helps build family pride.

166 ❤ Children's allowances must be big enough for them to buy something they value or they will lose interest. To encourage saving, it should not be enough to satisfy all urges.

167 ❤ Allow your children to make mistakes with money while they're young and the stakes are small.

168 ❤ Always pay allowances on the same day of the week, preferably at the same time of day.

169 ❤ Provide your children with a list of household responsibilities that are appropriate for their age. Make it clear exactly what is expected of them as family members.

170 ❤ Once your children are taking care of their family responsibilities, you can help them learn about working for money by giving them a chance to earn extra money doing special one-time jobs for the family.

171 ❤ No parenting technique works without love.

172 ❤ Children under twelve do extra tasks better if working for a lump sum rather than by the hour.

173 ❤ Kids under twelve shouldn't be given lunch money along with their allowance; a child this young is generally broke long before the school week is over.

174 ❤ Add an extra 20% to your child's allowance with the understanding that half is for savings and the other half for charity.

175 ❤ Pay your child's allowance by check. Teach them to go to the bank, where they can pay their savings account as they cash their check.

176 ❤ Charity is an important part of learning about money. Taking your children out where they will see real people in need is helpful in teaching the value of charity.

177 ❤ Teach your children that society's values can be different from traditional values.

178 ❤ Encourage your children to open a special savings account for any big ticket item. They could have one account for college, one for a special trip, and yet another for a car.

179 ❤ It now takes more money to amuse a child than it did to educate his or her parents.

180 ❤ Teach your kids all about money. Explain how interest works, tell them about the different kinds of bank accounts available, and show them how to read the financial pages in the daily newspaper.

181 ❤ Celebrate your child's strengths, no matter how small.

182 ❤ Praise builds self-esteem.

183 ❤ Value education.

184 ❤ Most children like to do nothing better than homework.

185 ❤ Teach your children to always walk facing traffic and that they should ride their bicycles in the same direction as traffic.

186 ❤ Never avoid questions about sex. It's important to give off the attitude that it's okay to ask questions about babies and bodies.

187 ❤ One of the most valuable skills you can teach boys or girls is cooking.

188 ❤ Preschoolers learn by watching.

189 ❤ Math can become real in the kitchen. You can teach kids fractions by letting them measure. Younger children can count cans.

190 ❤ Help your kids learn geography by requesting tourism information and sharing it with them.

191 ❤ Take your kids on tours of local businesses. They'll learn about all kinds of jobs and industries, and it will be useful in helping them to select a career.

192 ❤ Reward slow readers for each book read. It could be ice cream, baseball cards, or some other small item they would be willing to work for.

193 ❤ Teach your kids self-reliance and resourcefulness.

194 ❤ Share jokes.

195 ❤ Teach your kids how to whistle, or learn along with them.

196 ❤ Organize a group outing.

197 ❤ Pick dandelions with your kids.

198 ❤ Put family photos in albums together.

199 ❤ Play games with your kids but remember that winning is important for them too.

200 ❤ Watch a movie together.

201 ❤ Kids brighten up a home. The problem is they do it by leaving on all the lights.

202 ❤ Teach your children early in life to call home whenever they'll be late. You'll reap the benefits during the teenage years.

203 ❤ Encourage your kids to put on a play or invent a new game.

204 ❤ Write a family song.

205 ❤ When buying toy trains or remote control cars, you should always buy two. One for the child and another for their father.

206 ❤ Always have film in the camera.

207 ❤ If you have a pool, make sure it is fenced and locked.

208 ❤ Always start and end a correction with a positive statement. If the living room is a mess but the kids did turn off the TV, acknowledge that first.

209 ❤ Celebrate the good but recognize that there's always room for improvement.

210 ❤ With young children, completing the job is more important than how well the task is done.

211 ❤ Children are aware of their class standing. Guidance, not a lecture, is often the answer to poor grades.

212 ❤ Never turn down a hug.

213 ❤ Encourage your kids to conduct their own pre-election surveys.

214 ❤ Have a family "philosophical discussion" every Friday at dinner.

215 ❤ Hold fire drills and discuss two safe ways to exit each room. Practice emergency routines.

216 ❤ Sex education can be explained through books; ask your library for those that are appropriate to your child's age.

217 ❤ Help your child bake cookies.

218 ❤ Encourage your kids to write a neighborhood newsletter.

219 ❤ Teach your children not to procrastinate by showing them how to break down big jobs into a number of small tasks to reach their finished goal.

220 ❤ Explain to your children the link between doing well in school and their future lifestyle.

221 ❤ Teach your children what to do in case their clothing catches on fire. Instruct them to drop to the floor and roll over and over while protecting their face with their hands.

222 ❤ Tell your kids to stay away from fallen electrical lines.

223 ❤ Make sure your children know why they should stay away from power lines when flying a kite, or climbing a tree.

224 ❤ Instruct your kids to stay away from strange dogs and cats. Teach them never to disturb a dog that is sleeping or eating.

225 ❤ What parent ever has time for a crisis?

226 ❤ Children should be taught their address and phone number just as soon as they are able to remember them.

227 ❤ Tell your children that they should never hide under a bed or in a closet during a fire, so that adults can find them quickly.

228 ❤ Teach all your kids to sew.

229 ❤ Your child's education is much too important to be left solely up to school teachers.

230 ❤ Behavior change is best achieved through positive techniques rather than punishment.

231 ❤ Visual tours work well with preschool children. For example, you can teach them about history by taking them to visit museums or historic attractions.

232 ❤ Let someone else teach your teenager to drive, even if you have to exchange this chore with a neighbor.

233 ❤ Teach your children "oral contraception" — how to say no.

234 ❤ Adolescence is when kids stop asking questions because they know all the answers.

235 ❤ Teach your teenagers to change a tire before you teach them to drive.

236 ❤ Watch the election process and
results with your kids.

237 ❤ Teens often feel overloaded; evaluate
their schedule and help them to plan
their time.

238 ❤ Do something special with your
teenager. Attend a concert together.

239 ❤ *"What is childhood but a series of happy delusions."*

Sydney Smith

240 ❤ It's important for parents to take care of their health. After all, if you live a long life you'll eventually get the chance to be as big a pain to your kids as they were to you.

241 ❤ Why is it so hard to get kids into the bathtub when you can't keep them out of any other body of water?

242 ❤ Bubble gum has one big advantage: kids can't ask questions, or argue, while chewing it right.

243 ❤ Never swear at your kids.

244 ❤ Never give away your children's outgrown toys without their permission.

245 ❤ Compliment your kids every day.

246 ❤ It is easy to be a parent from a safe distance. Ignore remarks made by non-parents.

247 ❤ Just when you think your children never listen to the advice you're always handing out, you'll turn around to find them grown up and passing it on to their own children.

248 ❤ There's nothing quite like having children to make you realize it's a changing world.

249 ❤ In order for children to turn out right, a good parent sees to it they get everything that's coming to them, both good and bad.

250 ❤ Make a deal with your teenagers. Agree to stop doing one thing that annoys them if they will stop doing one thing that annoys you!

251 ❤ Let your children experience the thrill of doing things themselves. Sometimes nondirectional advice is better than giving orders. Try saying, "sometimes it helps if ...".

252 ❤ It is nearly impossible to be quiet when you have nothing to occupy your time.

253 ❤ When you allow your children to do as they please, you soon find yourself not pleased by anything they do.

254 ❤ If courtesy, generosity, honesty and thoughtfulness is not practiced at home, your child will never develop these positive traits.

255 ❤ I have yet to meet parents who practice everything they expect of their children.

256 ❤ Even the best parents sometimes raise their voices or lose control.

257 ❤ Everyone needs some time to do whatever pleases themselves.

258 ❤ For the first 30 years of your life you try to please your parents. You spend the rest of your life trying to please your kids.

259 ❤ If you do not respond to your child's bad behavior in a consistent manner, you can't expect to correct the problem.

260 ❤ Parents who are tempted to judge their child's playmates by their family should keep in mind that Cain came from a good one.

261 ❤ If you've said something you regret to your child, explain to him or her what made you get that angry, then apologize.

262 ❤ Those of you asking yourself if you're a good parent probably are. Bad parents don't care.

263 ❤ If you disapprove of something your children want, tell them why.

264 ❤ The problem is not the child, it's the behavior. React accordingly.

265 ❤ The President doesn't have a line
item veto, but parents do. Use it.

266 ❤ Teach your kids responsibility for their actions by accepting responsibility for your own.

267 ❤ Teach by example.

268 ❤ Take the time to listen to your children's feelings, perceptions and observations.

269 ❤ Before you encourage your children to learn a musical instrument, be sure you're willing to attend all of their concerts.

270 ❤ When a problem occurs in a group of kids, let the children decide how to handle the problem. Let them share the responsibility.

271 ❤ Use attention and praise to strengthen your child's good behavior.

272 ❤ The desire to do good, or harm, is most often a learned response. Look hard at family relations and you will most likely discover the root of your child's problem.

273 ❤ Teach youngsters how to use rewards to help themselves accomplish tasks.

274 ❤ Reinforce your child for trying, don't just recognize his or her failures.

275 ❤ Never accept abuse from your children. You don't have to.

276 ❤ Never keep a gun in the house if you have children in the house.

277 ❤ Don't compare your child, either positively or negatively, to others.

278 ❤ When assigning a chore always begin with the word "now", or another element of time.

279 ❤ Who can understand teenagers? They spend all day at school together yet can hardly wait to get home so they can call one another on the phone.

280 ❤ Those same teenagers are always too tired to hold a dish towel, but never too tired to hold the telephone.

281 ❤ Once your teenagers start to monopolize the telephone you'll wonder why you were so eager for them to say their first word.

282 ❤ Involve your kids in sports. A teenager who's out trying to steal second base doesn't have much time to steal cars.

283 ❤ A visit to a drug rehabilitation center, home for unwed mothers or to a hospital where drug-addicted babies can be viewed will leave a deeper impression on your children than all the lectures in the world.

284 ❤ Treat your children fairly and they will appreciate justice.

285 ❤ You have the right to be treated with courtesy and respect by your children. Demand it in a courteous and respectful way!

286 ❤ The person who designed portable radios that only work with headphones must have been a parent with teenagers in the car.

287 ❤ Teach your children to write thank-you notes.

288 ❤ Read to your children every day; they're never too young.

289 ❤ Make it easy for your children to take phone messages by leaving a pad and secured pen nearby.

290 ❤ Kids are a real comfort in your old age. This is good, since they help you to reach it faster.

291 ❤ Never allow phone calls during dinner.

292 ❤ Learn to say "thank you" and teach children to do likewise.

293 ❤ If you think your child hasn't learned the importance of an apology, you've never listened to how often they apologize to their friends for having such old-fashioned parents.

294 ❤ Encourage kids to do volunteer work in the community.

295 ❤ Children are born unique; do not expect them all to turn out the same.

296 ❤ It's impossible to treat all children equally.

297 ❤ Bringing up children by the book is fine as long as you realize you'll need a different book for each child.

298 ❤ Give your child the pleasure of pleasing you.

299 ❤ Good parents exercise constantly: they exercise self-control, tact and authority.

300 ❤ Don't expect more of your children than you gave as a child.

301 ❤ Decide now who should raise your kids in case of your demise.

302 ❤ Make a will.

303 ❤ Never spank a child when you're angry.

304 ❤ Set aside time for yourself.

305 ❤ Make grocery shopping a family experience. It's one of the best opportunities for teaching your children how to stretch a dollar.

306 ❤ Buy whatever your kids and their friends are selling.

307 ❤ Teach them the art of tipping.

308 ❤ Help your kids to be conscientious consumers. Make sure they learn the power of the boycott.

309 ❤ *"Every baby born into the world is a finer one than the last."*

Charles Dickens

310 ❤ By the time most people can really afford to have children they're already grandparents.

311 ❤ Attend all school functions.

312 ❤ Find out what makes each child unique and focus on those attributes.

313 ❤ Help your children to develop a strong sense of who they are.

314 ❤ Aggressive children who do not receive firm, but positive attention will often defy the law as adults.

315 ❤ Mothers appreciate the value of an education most when summer is over and children back in school.

316 ❤ Many people know time is money, but the best thing a parent can spend on their kids is not money, it's time.

317 ❤ Take a class with your kids.

318 ❤ Never let your child think you hate or resent him or her.

319 ❤ Listen for the feelings behind your child's words or anger.

320 ❤ You'll never convince a teenager that some day they'll be just as old-fashioned as their folks.

321 ❤ Use family dinners for togetherness not discipline.

322 ❤ The question is not whether one child has done as well as another, it's whether that child has done as well as he or she could.

323 ❤ Admit it when you're wrong.

324 ❤ Ask your child to lie for you and he or she will soon learn to lie to you.

325 ❤ Buckling your child's seatbelt takes a lot less time than waiting for the ambulance to arrive.

326 ❤ Children are like ideas; none are so wonderful as your own.

327 ❤ By the time you realize your parents were pretty smart you usually have kids who think you're pretty dumb.

328 ❤ Get down to eye level when speaking to children.

329 ❤ Prejudice is easily inherited and hard to erase. Don't teach it!

330 ❤ Recognize the difference between short-term, long-range and more important goals. Short term goals teach organization, long-range goals mold character, but the most important goal for parents is to provide a loving, supportive family.

331 ❤ Share your childhood fears.

332 ❤ Keep emergency phone numbers posted right beside the phone.

333 ❤ Express your anger responsibly.

334 ❤ When trying to gain control of your kids' misbehavior use a firm tone of voice and calmly point out what you expect done and when.

335 ❤ Non-assertive children who are not given the attention they need often end up as needy adults.

336 ❤ Before children reach their teens you spend a lot of time reminding them to turn off lights. After that you're more worried about why they have the lights turned off.

337 ❤ Close your arguments with a hug.

338 ❤ Accept your children for who they are, and they will find love in the world.

339 ❤ If you're not troubling your children when they are young, they'll be trouble when they grow up.

INDEX

Half Wisdom *Half Wit*

The User's Guide Series from One More Press

A USER'S GUIDE TO A BETTER BOD
Wisdom for Facing the Trials of Creating a Healthier, Happier You   ISBN 0-941361-96-9 $6.50

A USER'S GUIDE TO LIVING WITH PETS
Wisdom for Facing the Trials of Living with Dogs and Cats   ISBN 0-941361-95-0 $6.50

A USER'S GUIDE TO LOVE
Wisdom for Facing the Trials of Intimate Relationships   ISBN 0-941361-97-1 $6.50

A USER'S GUIDE TO MONEY
Wisdom for Facing the Trials of Making, Keeping and Spending It   ISBN 0-941361-94-2 $6.50

A USER'S GUIDE TO OLD AGE
Wisdom for Facing the Trials of Growing Older   ISBN 0-941361-98-5 $6.50

A USER'S GUIDE TO PARENTHOOD
Wisdom for Facing the Trials of Raising Kids   ISBN 0-941361-99-3 $6.50

These lighthearted books by Jo Elder and M.I. Wiser are available at bookstores and gift shops everywhere. If you are unable to find them locally, they may be ordered by mail from the publisher, One More Press, P.O. Box 1885, Lake Oswego, OR 97035. Please enclose a check or money order for the cost of the books plus $2.50 per order for shipping and handling.

ABOUT THE AUTHORS

Jo Elder and M.I.Wiser have spent the better part of two lifetimes handing out advice, in a style that's wise and witty.

Just like the readers of their **User's Guides** and popular advice column, *Half Wisdom / Half Wit*, Jo and M.I. have personally dealt with many of life's challenges. Between them, they've lived through two successful marriages and one bitter divorce. They've suffered the loss of close family members, fought and won the daily battle against weight gain and dealt with the problems involved in raising childen (and pets) in today's high-pressure world. Jo and M.I., who live in Oregon, have attended college, had successful careers and created profitable businesses. They are the authors of more than two dozen books.

Jo and M.I. like to think of their **User's Guides** as instruction manuals for surviving life's most common, but troublesome, situations.